T0208407

DARK DREAMS AND ANCIENT LULLABIES

FRANKIE BATZ

authorHOUSE

AuthorHouse™
1663 Liberty Drive
Bloomington, IN 47403
www.authorhouse.com
Phone: 1 (800) 839-8640

© 2020 Frankie Batz. All rights reserved.

No part of this book may be reproduced, stored in a retrieval system, or transmitted by any means without the written permission of the author.

Published by AuthorHouse 03/03/2020

ISBN: 978-1-7283-4957-2 (sc)
ISBN: 978-1-7283-4955-8 (hc)
ISBN: 978-1-7283-4956-5 (e)

Library of Congress Control Number: 2020904200

Print information available on the last page.

Any people depicted in stock imagery provided by Getty Images are models, and such images are being used for illustrative purposes only. Certain stock imagery © Getty Images.

This book is printed on acid-free paper.

Because of the dynamic nature of the Internet, any web addresses or links contained in this book may have changed since publication and may no longer be valid. The views expressed in this work are solely those of the author and do not necessarily reflect the views of the publisher, and the publisher hereby disclaims any responsibility for them.

Contents

When The Morning Comes

Lingered scent, from evenings past,
Surrounds me, in splendid misery
Life's enticing fragrance, dances in the air,
Arousing me from deaths eternal trance
A victim to my hungers will, I answer to its call,
To satisfy its lustful wants, desired from their flesh
Stirring the inner creature, waking from dormant dreams,
My craving aches, to greet the nights embrace
Silent winds of shadowed breath, obscure me from the light,
Taking flight, into the living realm
Waiting in the blackness, shrouded from their eyes,
I will feast unnoticed, drain them of their lives
Victim to my touch, silent scream erupts,
Pulsing warmth, invites me to indulge
Ravenous desire, rips flesh and devours,
Satisfy the inner beast, fulfillment comes at last
Piercing rays of gilded light, intrudes upon the dark,
Sending shadows, hurried into hiding
Blinded by its brilliance, the night begins to fade,
Now the morning comes, cursed be the light
Shield my eyes and shelter me, darkness take my hand,
Protect me, from the burning sight of day
Carry me to blissful sleep, retreating shadows cry,
Once again, I shall die, until the day subsides

Hidden Remains

Hidden from their icy stares,
My body rests in fear
Frenzied screams of howling wraith's,
Fly rampant in the air
Welcomed when I felt their touch,
Blood streams formed my name
Now that death has called me forth,
They search beneath each stone
Grisly smiles, reveal their hate,
These demons seek my corpse
Disturb the hallowed ground, I lie,
To take me into hell
The worms will pick my carcass clean,
Before they find my grave
Winter's frost, entombs my soul,
In hiding I remain

One More

In the lair of forgotten light,
The crimson shade respires
Bringing forth the silent end,
He's summoned from it's depths
A ghostly shadow, draped in night,
He rides the hidden winds
Fear his touch, in madness dream,
The hour glass runs dry
Dark entries fill the ancient book,
His list of names grows long
Empty eyes, gaze blankly still,
In hollowed, blackened sight
The fiendish smile that mortifies,
Haunts the nearing end
And one more name has been inscribed,
In the ledger of the dead

Night Song

Death looms in distant shadow
Patient, forever waiting its time
Complete and undisturbed, constant and unnerved
Truthful and pure in essence
Night's whispered song, sooths so sweet
A lullaby of restful sleep
Caressing you in blissful arms
Easing the pain of life's false dream
Peaceful release from one tender kiss
Softly, merging as one with the wind and night

One Hundred Years

Lying languished in a veil of blackened sorrow,
Its velvet touch drapes me in its wistful embrace
All is silent for one hundred years
The sleep of dreamers, invades the thoughts of desperation,
Cast the dust into my eyes, I'm blinded by the light
All is silent for one hundred years
Time's cruel vision takes hold of the present past,
Hours and days pass, I descend deeper into sleep
All is silent for one hundred years
A hunger breeds, a decaying heart erupts with hate,
The shadows cascade, spilling from a hollowed carcass
All is silent for one hundred years
The tears of angels, bathe me in contempt,
The loathsome cries of mourning sons, despise
And silence is shattered, awakening the dawning end

The Lover's Passion

In cold descent and blackened dreams,
My hunger turns to her
Her scent, it draws me out of hiding,
Desire burns for her
Penetrate her soul and flesh,
Her parted lips deceive
A hidden breath, a tortured smile,
This passion blazes dark
The shadows bleed in misery,
Tear drops turn to dust
Serenades of withered moans,
Stalked by dark delights
Released unto the moonlit night,
My lover's passion cries
From scarlet stains, bloom moon kissed dreams,
In darkness, now she waits

Silent Screams

Shallow graves, fiendish plots,
Shameless and revealed
Maimed and dragged, earth is dug,
Silent screams muffled by death
Empty eyes, frozen cold,
Lifeless and betrayed
Bound and gagged, drenched in blood,
Silent screams trapped in her head
Stolen souls, tortured flesh,
Nameless and defaced
Bagged and tagged, covered in mud,
Silent Screams plead for revenge
Spirits roam, drifting free,
Restless and disturbed
Lost and found, caked in crud
Silent screams cry for release
Gathered slaves, twilight burns,
Endless and defiled
Hidden by shadows, crimson tides flood,
Silent screams captured forever

FREEZER BURN

Frozen in silence, a crystallized tomb,
The shadowless ones bid me sleep
Trapped all alone, the nightmare begins,
I beg for this dream to now end
Horror and torment reside in my mind,
Suspended in time's icy grip
Slowly it creeps, the cold takes its hold,
Life and death one in the same
Mummified in this thermal embrace,
A future rebirth, known not to me
Created by science, confined in this grave,
An eternal breath, I will forever hold

World's End

Through the tears of a dying world,
The pleading children cry
Fed upon by swirling vultures,
Their prayers of hope denied
Raging winds of poisoned doom,
Bellow forth the end
Released to conquer and destroy,
The horsemen's wrath descends
Plague and famine, war and death,
Thunder cross the lands
The truth of life is raped and torn,
Consumed by that which kills
Severed dreams drift aimlessly,
Scattered in the winds
Delirium's confused descent,
Draws madness from its lair
From bloodied lips, a stench so foul,
The final answer spoke
The last remains of man's decline,
Lie buried in the dust

Minion

Church bell rings with urgency,
The rain, like needles fall
All are safe, behind locked doors,
In distance, hear it's call
Crawling towards the edge of town,
Its shadow takes its flight
Blotting out the moonlit sky,
Its evil rules this night
Slipping under broken seal,
The air is vapid dust
Seeping into mortal flesh,
Lost souls, they rot and rust
Blasphemer of the holy truth,
Deceiver of the weak and frail
Heed its uttered whisper,
On winds of silent call
The beast has cast its evil spell,
Flames dance with the crashing stars
Time of ruin is at hand,
On earth as it is in hell

Civilized

In a careless world filled with pain,
Violence finds its place
Upon the pillars of false pride,
Rest the ones impaled with lies
They are civilized
Technodreams, corrupt with disease,
The mindless stumble and fall
Harvester's of the human flesh,
The king of filth, reigns with blinded eyes
They are civilized
Wasted hearts believe in the end,
Armageddon is an answered prayer
Eyeless children, jump into the flames,
Feel their terror, hear their sullen cries
This is civilized

ABRACADAVER

The rose that blooms at midnight,
Warns of the coming dread
Drenched in crimson moonlight,
Comes the waking of the dead
Witches mate with hellish demons,
Lost souls are called from death
Ancient winds of perverse seasons,
Give back the dead's last breath
Rotted stench defiles the air,
The crimson night has fallen
Invoked by magic, demon's stare,
They answer to his calling
Risen corpses roam the night,
Birthed from the mud
In service to the lord of light,
They feast on flesh and blood

Forever

Haunted by her memory, driven half insane,
A growing madness, infects his torrid mind
Ghastly thoughts are hidden, from unsuspecting eyes,
Tortured by the love he's lost, reclaiming her tonight
Kneeling down before her grave, digging up the earth,
Guided by his ghoulish needs, united with the night
Defiling all that's sacred, he longs to set her free,
To hold her as his lover, for all eternity
Through splintered wood and ashened earth, she's finally revealed,
Wrapped in soiled linens, aged by the passing time
Still intact, he pulls her up, from her rest disturbed,
Hollowed eyes and cold dead lips, blankly silent, still
Held in tender arms, she limply dangles free,
Her brittle flesh so mildewed and decayed
A romance now renewed, exploring hands insist,
The sickly grin of frozen death, greets his probing eyes
White pain bursts within his head, fingers pierce his brain,
Her icy grasp, forever holds him near
Bound to her eternally, a spell he cannot break,
Her whispered song, drifts gently on the wind

Succubus

On the wings of ravens, her breath descends,
With gentle wisps of fragrant wind
A silent touch, against my cheek,
She slips, into my darkest dreams
Luminous eyes, impale my vacant spirit,
With the gaze of a thousand lost days
Aroused from the depths of secret sins,
Restless wants, stir deep inside
Her sultry scent, commands my thoughts,
Lust rules my weakened mind
Caressed and inflamed, by magenta kisses,
Enslaved, by ravenous pleasures
Forever bewitched, by her timeless beauty,
I'm her offering to the night
A fresh flesh that is devoured and scourged,
With passion's touch, we burn
My weeping body is stripped and defaced,
Engulfed with the cravings of death
I bleed the tears of eternal damnation,
Her teasing laughter, echoes, deep within

Dark Dreams and Ancient Lullabies

Cradled in its cold embrace,
The night begins to fall
Haunting every sleeping moment,
Dreams of death prevail
Drifting through the midnight mist,
Eerie music plays
Melodies of distant calling,
Familiar, yet so strange
Broken and distorted,
Embedded in my brain
Shattered notes, piercing sleep,
Like shards of splintered glass
The voices now invade my mind,
In a chorus so deranged
Beckon me out from the darkness,
Driving me insane
Insomniac or maniac,
Confusion takes its hold
Peering eyes and tainted smiles,
Fade in and out of view
Horror becomes my master,
And to its call I wake

Manifested dreams are real,
All hope for rest is lost
Chanting grows in fevered pitch,
Insidious in nature
Compelling me to rise and answer,
But I am dead within this grave

Pity Me

Look into my eyes, see the horror that is me,
Condemned to live in darkness, for all eternity
Lifeless as the shadows, tortured is my sleep,
In silence I do suffer, the tears of woe, I weep
Embraced by all that's evil, it gave this curse to me,
I pass my time in loneliness, I wish to be set free
A servant to the blackness, a slave to my disease,
A hunger stirs deep within, that which I must please
Damned by its desires, I beg for my release,
Plunge the wood within my chest, offer me my peace

Into The Mirror Black

It has been said, magic was born,
Beyond the great mountains of dread
Phantoms and demons dwell in the winds,
Protecting the rarest of finds
Thousands have fallen, seeking out knowledge,
Its powers too strong to resist
Corpses lie bloodied, stripped of their flesh,
A warning of impending doom
None are discouraged, the pathway's obscured,
Cluttered with putrid remains
The winds bow in reverence, with his approach,
The master of mystical light
Dancing stars, swirl in his hands,
His footsteps beckon up flame
Seeking the legend, the mirror of black,
That which was forged in the pit
Encrusted with emeralds, carved out of stone,
Its surface shimmers and flows
Hidden in darkness, buried by time,
Its call draws him closer to death
Nightmares unleashed, the fading day cries,
The skies echo thunderous screams
Held in his grip, the mirror glows red,
Eternity's end soon will come
Mystical realms invoke dark illusions,

Drawing him deep in its gaze
Reflections are lost, shadows disperse,
Trapped, he is taken beyond
Revealed is the powers of magical sight,
The pains of a thousand dark years
Into the mirror, forever he'll live,
Taunted by the specters of night

Four

A longing expectation, of past beliefs be known,
Prophecies deliberately revealed
Preordained and destined fate, awoken realm released,
Sending forth annihilation's dream
Famine, war, death and plague, take to open skies,
With mighty steeds of raging thunder ride
Assembled on the mount of skulls, four have set the pace,
Plotting out the end of days for man
Fulfilling that which was predicted, this genocide begins,
Lay waste the world with misery and pain
One by one nations fall, starvation sweeps the lands,
Winds of sickness carry with it death
Crops rot in the burning sun, oceans turn to blood,
Decaying bloated bodies litter streets
Cleansed and disinfected, worldwide slaughter is done,
In silence four retreat into the night

Till Death

[edit]

Your name rests upon my lips,
Never to be spoken
Images of who you were,
Linger in my mind
Now your breathless corpse,
Lies in crated stillness
Waiting for the moon to set you free
This hour that approaches,
Sunlight greyly dims
Draining all the color from the day
With each passing moment,
Fear consumes my soul
Madness soon shall wake from death's black sleep
And with the faith of angels,
Dark demons at my back
I dare to face the one that I once loved

Sentinels of Darkness

Way beyond the moon that wanders,
The gates of twilight stand
Silent whispers, fallen dreams,
The winds of sanity cry
Guardians of the blackest stone,
Protect the realm of night
Omnipotent and pitiless,
They watch the passing time
Future's past collides with now,
Stardust swirls and strays
Threatened by the days approach,
Hostile winds blow forth
Sentinels of darkness rise,
To face the nights enemy
Shade and light, entwine in battle,
Fighting for tomorrow
Captured time writhes in agony,
Despondent and confused
Withered light, turns to black,
The shattered day retreats
The lingered remnants of broken shadows,
Return, to night's tranquil arms

Morbid Tales

Weave a tale of morbid thoughts,
Fabricate the truth
Entice them with your nimble tongue,
Draw them closer to doom
Flames accentuate your words,
Dancing shadows speak
Light and dark entwine as one,
Story time's begun
Ancient beasts and tortured dreams,
Corrupt the infant mind
Introduce the laughing night,
The tale begins to breathe
Terror slowly clings and claws,
Embracing all that's feared
Teeter on the edge of sanity,
Anticipate the end
Caught within the fabled lies,
Tangles up in dread
A bedtime friend that suffocates,
Resides in tortured sleep

BLACK REIGN

The stars cascade, from a shattered sky,
Frozen, are the stagnant tides
A bloodied moon, burns and dies,
The planets are aligned
Foretold in the book of truth,
Its coming does draw near
The seal upon the gate is broken,
Set free, are the legions of hell
Withered and forsaken, submissive and despised,
Carrion of a dying race, decays to putrid ruin
Flames of blasphemy, consume the ashen lands,
Tenebrion, cast's all into the darkest night
The waking night, breeds and spreads,
Birthing the newly created
Condemning all to a tortured existence,
Suffering in the blackest light
Abaddon's armies, cast their spell,
Carnage and death, their trophies are souls
The fierceness of hell, transforms his world,
All is lost, within his blackened pain
The blood is spilled, the altar's set,
The master takes complete control
Power's of the sinful one, revealed to the coming son
…And the prophecy is fulfilled

Apartment 213

A chamber of horrors, a place filled with death,
A workshop of deviant art
Dahmer the wicked, the sinister beast,
In madness, he stalks through the night
Seduction his ploy, the trap has been set,
Willing, they put up no fight
Locking the door, nowhere to run,
Tricked into being his prey
Consumed by his urges and sexual needs,
Torture and death become one
Bloodshed and mayhem, cannibal rites,
Indulge in the flesh of the dead
Freezing their heads, collecting their bones,
Possessing them body and soul
Raping the carcass, stewing the meat,
Preserving his victims in jars
The stench of decay, a demon at play,
Skulls are his trophies of choice
The world of a madman, a psychotic fiend,
Resides behind door 213

Black Science

Mengele's children suffered and bled,
Tortured, for the good of the cause
Genetic freaks discarded like filth,
Altered, unto the likeness of death
Two by two, the twins were led,
Shackled, by identical lives
Disfigured by the scars of hatred,
Black science, damned their souls
Manipulate the gift of thought,
Progress, deviates our existence
Reproduce the birth of man,
Extinguish his imperfect past
Genetically pure, a race will evolve,
Replacing the ones that still live
Twins will be led, but one will survive,
Soulless, his eyes scan the world
Discarded as filth, a race filled with fault,
The furnaces burn once again
Exterminate, this genetic disease,
Make way for the replicant race
Claiming our lives, cursing our dreams,
A new age of man will begin
God becomes myth, labs become wombs,
Black science, will damn all our souls

Children of Madness

War torn streets, raised in fear,
The laughter is silenced forever
Bloody rivers flow and subside,
Memories of pain still remain
A childhood filled with shattered beliefs,
Youth sacrificed to the fight
Born to a world of political strife,
They take to the shadows and hide
A conflict based on hate and tradition,
A generation's evils are passed
Infest the minds and lives of the young,
A legacy of madness is theirs
Laid to rest in a nameless grave,
Dreams mold and rot in the mud
Scarred by the horrors of blistering fires,
Convulsing minds are destroyed
Slaughtered and maimed, are the bed time rhymes,
Happy endings, rewritten by death
Tear stained diaries, weathered by time,
Silk draped bodies pile high
All are forgotten by the wagers of war,

The children of madness are lost
A future uncertain, blinded by rage,
Casualties tossed in the void
In the name of the past, all hope is forsaken,
Giving birth to a warring race
Condemned to repeat their father's mistakes,
They'll teach their offspring well

No Name Maddox

Nameless at birth, a monster was born,
A bastard son, abused
With criminal mind and deranged thought,
Imprisoned, in his youth
Half his life, spent behind bars,
A masterful liar, released
In the summer of Love, the Haight became home,
Wielded his spell of deceit
The prophet, of Armageddon had come,
Bearing the gifts of false dreams
Society's children, waited for answers,
They clung to the words that he spoke
This Devil-Christ figure, preyed on their hopes,
Claiming them body and soul
Considered divine, his grip became strong,
Recruited the young, for his deeds
Twisted their minds, transformed their wills,
A death squad, prepared for attack
Deep in the night, the devil roamed free,
Murder and death were unleashed
Written in blood, a war was declared,
Six slaughtered, at Cielo drive
Panic swept through the Hollywood hills,
The family killed once again
Two more were butchered, chaos ensued,

Sacrificed, for his psychotic cause
Joining the list, of the criminally insane,
His name will forever be cursed
Safely locked tight, the god of fuck rots,
Charles Manson, is nameless no more

Moonfire

Something wicked rules the night,
A nightmare that roams free
None are safe when darkness falls,
This creature seeks out blood
Howling haunts the misty moors,
The crimson moon burns bright
The bane that blooms with cursed rage,
Calls out the beast that lurks
Tortured violence, piercing screams,
The darkened skies grows cold
Blood flows sweet, flesh turns pale,
Steaming entrails burst
The hunger of the beast's fulfilled,
Another victim falls

Faust

Tortured nightly, hear them scream,
The voices of the damned
Within the shadows thickened mist,
Laughter mocks his fate
Made the choice, a bargain sealed,
A godless pact signed in blood
A thirst for knowledge and desire,
Cursed his mortal soul
Demonic guide so putrid and vile,
The smell of sin on his breath
Enticed with pleasures of the flesh,
The love for one was tainted
Unraveled dreams and scandalous shame,
His life left in ruin from grace
For twenty four years, the hour draws near,
Mephisto, gloats with delight

A Monster Be Damned

Midnight desecration, disturbance of the dead,
Gathering of bodies, unholy acts of dread
Fresh flesh for his choosing, piled up in his lab,
Experiment nearly completed, lying on the slab
Assembled to his liking, the only of its kind,
Blasphemous creation, contains a criminal's mind
The waking of a new dawn, science bless his name,
Creature forced to accept life, exist's in cursed shame
Birthed by its deranged god, corrupted by his pride,
The ways of man are cruel, let madness be its guide
Horrific and disfigured, a souless beast now breathes,
Abandoned by its father, a contemptuous life it leads
Life bestowed upon the dead, awaits its welcomed grave,
Cast into the darkness, a victim and a slave,
With vengeful wrath, the blood of innocence flows,
Cursing its creator, to suffer the fits of woe
Caressed by his creation, an experiment gone awry,
Damned by its existence, this wretched monster dies
Walking into ice and snow, an avalanche descends,
The peace of death delivered, fate seals their dismal end

New World Order

Time has come, the nations of the world will cry out,
Beast of deceit, echoes his message throughout
Land of limbo, ruled by chaos and fear,
Heed the word, the coming of death draws near
New world order, established in the name of world peace,
One disorder, freedom and pride will soon cease
The sinner's are rewarded, the saints march off to their death's,
Slaves are we all, cowering to their threats
Innocent blood, drips from the palms of their hands,
Silenced cries, muffled in a Godless land
Bodies on bodies, pile up in communal graves,
Brutal black troops, claim the power they crave
The stench of rotting death, fills a stagnant air,
Life's reality, turns into a hellish nightmare
Violence and bloodshed, kill the mild and the meek,
Blackened oblivion, feeds off the weak
World consumed by hatred, fueled by the fires of sin,
A swirling storm of chaos, is ready to begin
Skies are blackened, oceans are poisoned and burn,
Condemned to relive history, what have we learned
Apocalyptic laughter, from the demon's in wait,
Impious and flawed, rise the offspring of hate

Queen of Blasphemy

Gaze upon her frozen stare,
The queen, she sleeps in silence
Sealed alone inside her tomb,
She waits for their arrival
Children born of blackest night,
They gather in the flames
Whispered echo, lying dormant,
They wait for her to wake
Deep within its eerie gaze,
The moonlight bathes her form
Touched by death, trapped in time,
Eternal damnation, her curse
In ancient phrase, her name is spoke,
Exhumed is the soul of black sin
The shadows rejoice as she wakes,
The queen has been released
The venom of darkest creation,
The mist of ages swirl
Her gifts shall be of woe and death,
Cast upon the Earth
Her reign will be so splendid,
She'll tear this world apart
Into the wind, her minion's take flight,
Her evil will be known
And all that stands will be destroyed,
By the Queen of Blasphemy

CREATURE FEATURES

Late night thriller,
Television scream
Morbid fascinations,
Lost within a dream
Radiating, sickly blue,
A hiss from far beyond
Captivate the senses dull,
The glow of death is fond
Visionary, skeptic run,
Ghoulish host spreads fear
Ugly faces shatter night,
These things are held so dear
Memories of giant beings,
Nucleic acid rains
Rising spirits from the dead,
Laughter so insane
Shadows dance across the wall,
Creatures from the grave
Festival of horror wails,
Sit still and be brave
Missing is the late night thrill,
Black and white attack
Monster's of my childhood dream,
Bring creature features back

5:38

Sleep eludes me, thoughts drift crazed,
I grasp for the chance to dream
Frozen time, no rest for me,
Each day begins the same
5:38 burns in my brain,
Consistent and submissive
I am slave to its haunting return,
Cursed, by its constant reminder
Surrounded by shadows, touched by its chill,
Repeating each day as the last
Caught in a limbo, a terror revealed,
5:38 marks the time of my death

Sanctum Santorum

Cursed by morning's early rise,
Held captive by its reign
Wandered dreams, my mind can't bare,
Dawn's gilded torment burns
Frozen by the touch of time,
In sleep, my sorrow screams
Confined in the darkest shadow,
Hidden from all light
The sanctuary of my rest,
In burial I lie
Kissed by Phagendena,
With lips of marble cold
I retreat into her arms,
Until the day subsides
The hunger stirs with savage lust,
My time of waking nears
I welcome night's exquisite touch,
My restless spirit roams

ᴎEVER

[edit]

Kept in silence, broken trance,
A Siren held in chains
Tongue removed, muscles twitch,
And never shall she speak
Gruesome grin, unmoving stare,
Disturbed but not distracted
Fastened tight, lips sealed shut,
And never shall she scream
Entombed within, kept from light,
Shrouded in her evil
Deathly praise, a song unheard,
And never shall she sing

TV Profit

Place your hands upon the screen,
Beg for your redemption
Miraculous, he'll save your soul,
The promise of Heaven awaits
Bathed in its healing light,
His words transcend the truth
Blinded by the faith he offers,
Forgiveness has its price
A culprit of the pulpit,
Sincerity, is what he lacks
Divinity is just a ploy,
Now pay for your salvation
Syndicated messiah, preys upon the weak,
To mesmerize and victimize, in the name of God
The crippled walk, the sightless see,
Hallelujah, one and all
Write your checks and send them fast,
Insufficient funds, result in damnation

Children Shouldn't Play
With Dead Things

Enticed by its dark mysteries,
Drawn to its whispered call
The secrets of the night,
Are better left alone
Entranced by its false promise,
You dare to play its game
Its words of invitation,
Are better left unheard
Gathered round the place of mourning,
Curse its sacred domain
Break the earth and desecrate,
This site of morbid dreams
Disturb his hallowed sleep,
Exhume his rotted bones
Light the candles, scream its name,
Provoke it out of hiding
Urge the winds to sing your praise,
Unanswered are your plea's
Mock the unseen with irreverence,
You ridicule its wrath
Childish in your tantrum,
The darkness slowly creeps
Waking from its blackened rest,
The shadows come alive
Bestowing life unto the dead,

Its vengeance shall be known
The earth erupts, corpses rise,
Fall down to your knees
With widened eyes and shallow breath,
You'll meet a fitting end
Frozen children, gripped in fear,
Playtime's master descends
Slaughtered and devoured,
By what the night does bring
The aftermath of scornful sin,
Children shouldn't play with dead things

Annihilation

From the ashes of a tragic past,
Comes the dawning of our end
Sanctified by blood and hate,
Wakes the nightmare blessed by man
With saddened eyes, the angel's weep,
The Heavens scorn its name
Breeding what was meant to be,
It hungers for our deaths
Spawned from man's conflicted will,
Feeding off his rage
Imminent, its rise has come,
And war shall be its name
Merciless, its heart beats blind,
Destructive and insane
Seething with the blood of torment,
The winds of death roam free
Blackened world, diseased remains,
Poisoned by its hand
All is dust and ashen waste,
Mankind's final shame

One Mind

Lost in loneliness, exiled from home,
Escaped the genocide of his race
Forced to find sanctuary, on a nameless sphere,
Aimlessly roaming this silent, barren land
Orange sand, burning suns, exotic creatures of oddity,
Death may have been a better fate then this
Trying to find solace in the nearing night,
Weary sleep, shattered by intruding thoughts
Screams of violent torture, tear at his brain,
Converging, melding seeping into his being
Writhing in pain, experiencing the death of millions,
Twisting, molding him into their savior supreme
Telepathic race, lives inside the mind of one,
Left to wander this land, in compete, utter madness

Nocturna Divine

Tragedy did take her life,
On winds of blackened whispers
Pulling her into the shadows,
Devouring her virgin soul
Ice cold granite marks the place,
The place in which she lies
Her presence lingers in the air,
Her scent, so pure and sweet
Haunting me, she calls my name,
The darkness breaths with life
Frozen eyes stare from beyond,
In sleep, they mesmerize
In spectral trance, she walks the night,
Her cravings strong with hunger
Crimson drips upon her breast,
Nocturnal feast, devours
Approaching in silence, her gaze so cold,
Captures my desires, takes hold of my soul
Embraced by death, a kiss like fire,
Our hearts are entwined in the blackness of sorrow
Together we lay, forever we sleep

CURSED REVENGE

Ancient sands, blow with rage,
The crypt has been defiled
Within the tomb, the watcher wakes,
A souless corpse, arise
Unleashed from his eternal sleep,
His blackened eyes stare wide
Servant to the pharaoh child,
In life, as well as death
Avenge this deed against the king,
A curse passed down through time
Bursting through the chamber walls,
His wrath, severe and swift
One by one, the guilty fall,
Their heart's ripped from their chest's
Crush their bodies into dust,
His judgment has been passed

THE JOINING

Erotic dreams, you've beckoned me,
To gratify your lust
From the shadows of the blackest depths,
I slip into your mind
Embraced in my salacious grip,
To take you is my right
Touch your skin, I make you moan,
Your inner cravings stir
Flames ignite your wanting needs,
Desire's passions flow
Your burning thighs, they welcome me,
In ecstasy you writhe
The pleasure's of the flesh are sweet,
Enticing is your taste
In my eyes, you see the truth,
Hypnotic is my stare
I've answered all your invitations,
Your carnal pleasures filled
Now offer me what is most sacred,
Join me now as one
Give me your life, sacrifice your blood,
Let me guide you past the veil of dreams
Pulse against my lips, agony arise,
A stinging kiss, forever you are mine
Lifeless in my arms, the chill of death awakes,
My bride in black, we'll desecrate the night

KILLER CLOWN

Strapped down to the table, with his life he'll pay,
A killer of the vilest kind, will burn in hell and rot
Sixteen years of justice, his sentence handed down,
Shed no tears of sorrow, for the killer clown
His mind contained thoughts so deranged, crazed and half insane,
He robbed the lives of thirty three and buried their remains
To Decompose and putrefy, underneath his home
Strangulate and suffocate, he tortured them for fun,
Trophies of his killing spree, rotting in the mud
No remorse or guilt was his, deviance his pleasure,
Added to the list of fiends, he's bearer of the crown
Shed no tears of sorrow, for the killer clown

COUNTESS BLOOD

Obsessed by her beauty, the Countess mad and crazed,
Reflected in her mirror black, the hands of time will fade
Sadistic and deranged, she seeks the gift of life,
To resurrect the years gone by and fight the aging days
Summoned to her sleeping chamber, a servant child disrobes,
Tender flesh so warm and smooth, arouses inner lusts
Passion's kiss is welcomed, by trembling lips so full,
Defiled by death's cold embrace, she cowers in her fear
Crimson fire burns with rage, behind her frenzied gaze,
Drawing blood so innocent, the countess laughs insane
Smearing life so pure and free, upon her wrinkled skin,
Tortured and impaled, the slaughtered corpses lie
Immersed in blood of virgin's fair, she baths among the dead
Enraptured in demented bliss, the screams of horror, sing

49

The King Must Die

A plot has been devised, in secret it remains,
Relieve him of the crown and strike him dead
Assassin's at the ready, waiting for the sign,
Bring him to his knees and end his reign
No one can be trusted, his paranoia grows,
The eyes of treason haunt him in his sleep
The royal throne is tarnished, corrupted and maligned,
Madness dictates reason through his deeds
The future of the country is at stake
An insane madman tempts his very fate
Through poisoning or by blade
This tyrants name will fade
The king must die and justice shall prevail
Forcibly dethroned, through the halls he screams,
The winds of revolution grow with rage
Bound by rusted chains, his scepter has been claimed,
The headsman's ax is sharpened for the kill
Betrayed by his first born, his ugly soul is cursed,
His final hours quickly pass him by
The kiss of death is swift, royal blood rains down,
Held high his head a symbol for the free

This Demon

Haunted by its cold black gaze,
It lingers by my side
At odds with the angels,
Its curses my beliefs
From my bones, my flesh is torn,
Holes burn in my mind
Tortured by its constant stare,
Restless is my will
Crawling from the shadows,
It slowly takes its place
It offers me its madness,
Reveals its blackest dream
Enraptured by its empty lies,
Consumed by its fiery touch
Embers is my withered soul,
Smoldering out existence
Taking leave, I am replaced,
Held captive by its scorn
This demon, screams in triumph,
This demon, now is me

ΠOSFERATU

Waiting for the sun to set, so I may rise again
To walk among the living and claim them for the dead
I travel in the shadows and prey upon their fears
Soon I'll get just what I need and pick their bodies clean
Glowing eyes will meet your gaze, your rapid pulse will cease
Still beating heart within my grasp, an orgiastic feast
The wind whispers my name, the earth, trembles and shakes
All life will cease, when its my time to wake
The moon will turn to blood, the sea's will turn to ice
Beware what the night will bring, I rule all that I please

Antichrist

Master of oblivion, creator of lost souls,
Tears apart the wills of weakest man
The bringer of the world's demise,
Contagion filled with wrath,
A birthed beast in common skin shall rise
Plagues of past prediction, Infest the present day,
Destroyers of humanity unleashed
Abysmal horrors feeding freely,
Torments madness screams,
Angelic wings engulfed in flames of lies
Gods have been abandoned, faithless and afraid,
Survivors are engulfed by darkest night
Withered spirits burn in fire,
Apocalypse brought forth,
Dominion of the netherworld be praised

Book of Shadows

Scribbled thoughts stain the pages,
Confessions written in blood
Diagrams of dark dementia,
Drip between the lines
Tales of perversion, madness screams,
Murderous deeds are disclosed
Unashamed pleasures, detailed accounts,
Numerous acts so deranged
A psychopath's triumph, secrets so foul,
A black, morbid glimpse into hell
Unraveled dreams, of deviante sex,
Entombed in the fabric of hate
Page upon page, the shadows emerge,
Souls of the dead trapped in time
Sadistic entries, conjure their deaths,
Condemned, to relive evil's crimes

Dead Girls Don't Say No

In the dark, my madness frowns,
The night plays wicked games
The restless breeze, in agony,
Whispers unto me
Deeply seized, my haunting cries,
The shadows take me forth
My worthless soul, in misery,
Answers to her call
Secret desires, not my own,
Moonlit nightmares revealed
Corrupted, by her wanting need,
Passion sets me free
Seduced by death, her spirit moans,
Invites me to her chamber
A silent kiss, in ecstasy, screaming out my name
Scorching moon, burns twice as bright,
A withered embrace takes me down
Defile her body, in blasphemy,
Dead girls don't say no

Cthulhu Rise

Moonbeams dance on the swirling tides,
Foaming tongues lick the shore
Beneath the waves, so violently stirs,
The madness from the sea
Spawned amongst the malevolent stars,
An ancient god dreams, tempestuously
Invading the minds of an infantile race,
Hideous shadows converge
And on the night winds, its name echoes far,
Shining eyes peer from the deep
Entombed within the ruins of time,
A slithering nightmare awakes
The rising of R'lyeh, the coming of doom,
Cthulhu's released from its sleep
Thick stench of death roams in the breeze,
Its bellowing roar, chills the air
Membranous wings, blot out the sun,
The horrors of evil revealed
Voraciously feeding, insanity cries,
To madness, the world will succumb

Into The Unknown

Afraid to close my eyes at night,
I fear what I might see
Haunted by her emerald eyes,
She tortures all my dreams
An ancient queen of evil pleasures,
A temptress dressed in black
Dissects my mind and steals my thoughts,
And hides them in dark places
An undead soul that wanders free,
She sings me songs of death
Her whispered chill, surrounds my soul,
Her icy glare burns fierce
Her wicked power's forged in the blackness,
Blessed by unholy rites
Invites the shadows to descend,
To drag me straight to hell
Held captive by her binding spell,
Madness takes its hold
She waits for me to take her hand,
Into the dark unknown

Temples of Ice

The perils of my quest be known, appear before my eyes,
Haunted shadows speak to me as one
Taunted on my journey, plagued by unseen foes,
Apparitions move amongst the winds
Dark dreams steal my courage, I must travel on,
To reach the fabled temples of black ice
Many souls have ventured, but none have graced their halls,
None have found the treasures they contain
Fallen by the wayside, entombed by frozen death,
Victims to the creeping shadows failed
Onward through the icy paths, tormented by their screams,
Specter's of forgotten kingdoms rage
Howling winds of madness, dare me to turn back,
I must fulfill the prophecies of time
Crystal spires prick the sky, made of blackest night,
The hour of my fate will soon arrive
A black cloaked mystic meets my gaze, bidding me to enter,
Guiding me on to my destiny
Wraiths of darkest evil, bow down as I pass,
Morbid hymns profess my rightful place
The magus of fallen desires, welcome me with praise,
The depths of darkness shudder at my feet

ReBiRTh

I reign beyond oblivion, I rule the nameless night,
I've returned to sit upon my throne
All mankind will be enslaved, I'll pick their carcass raw,
Their blood will flow like tepid soured wine
And when the twilight fades, blackest night remains,
And freezing death will be unleashed on all

REBIRTH

In rippled silence, night descends,
A veil of blackness shines
Amongst the dreams of sullen sleep,
The howling winds divide
Deep within the swirling mist,
Murmured voices conspire
Nameless nightmares rise and call,
Their deafened whisper roars
Blotting out the moon filled sky,
Ravenous shadows take flight
To feed upon this quiet splendor,
The eyes of horror stare
Entranced by that which has no name,
Its cold embrace endures
Drifting silent, through the breeze,
Death's welcomed kiss departs
The cup of life forlorn and stained,
Black serenades sing sweet
The mysteries of far beyond,
Revealed in one last breath
Suffered sleep creeps through dead bones,
The waking dawn turns black
Through the eyes of infant sight,
A world of shadow reigns

A child eternal born through death,
Caressed by nights cold hand
Walk amongst the clan of darkness,
The dreams of madness fade
Step inside the realm of twilight,
Hallowed by thy grave

Sinful

Feel what hungers inside you,
It lingers deep in your soul
Give into your desires,
Now it takes full control
Feel it in your mind,
Blackness sets in your heart
Consumed by madness' fire,
It rips your soul apart
Velvet hand of darkness,
Muffles screams of pain
Lying dormant in your soul,
Awakes the man insane
Heed the call of the banshee,
Drawn to its every word
Feeding off your weakness,
Step inside your grave

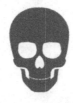

Videodrome

The gaze of static, pulses the mind,
Lures you into its grip
Drawn to its perverse display,
The TV never lies
Butchery of soft smooth flesh,
Blood red walls divine
Welcome to the truth made real,
Welcome to videodrome
Evil creation, mutation of soul,
Mind and body will follow
Lead you to the path of madness,
On your knees, you'll fall
Assassin emerges, the image controls,
A visual virus corrupts
Target the threat, annihilate truth,
Oblivion's daughter must die
Mission aborted, the master now bleeds,
Destroyed, by its own creation
A breathing screen, subliminal dreams,
A televised rebirth
Leave the flesh of old behind,
Accept the truth at last
Ascend beyond the confines of body,

Transmission of spirit will rise
The end of conspiracy, flesh is made new,
Submissive rule withers and dies
Death to the lies and falsehood's projected,
Death…to videodrome

Golden Dawn

Cast outside the realm of twilight,
Cursed by the confines of time
Banished from the world of light,
The want of knowledge, his crime
A Judas to the myth of man,
Betrayer of the Sacred word
Blackness and light, reigned by his hand,
The balance of nature, disturbed
Alchemist of word and thought,
Manipulator of sense
Minions of shadow, he has brought forth,
To aid in his defense
He ushers in the golden dawn,
Stars dance within his grasp
Thirteen stand, the shadows inflamed,
Invoking the beast from the pit
Chants are phrased in his dark name,
Demons invade flesh and feast
Orgy of carnal delights ensues,
Devoured in the lust of blood
Semen and fire, tangled in crimson hues,
Torments abound, upon its waking flood
Mist subsides, the shadows retreat,
The seeds are blessed by his word
The nectar of death tastes se sweet,
Nocturnal damnation unfurled

Walpurgis Night

Dark winds speak in subtle tones,
The church bell rings in fear
The chill of coming dread descends,
The sun sets black and hides
Shadows dance, the dead romance,
Crimson eyes peer forth
Witches drink the blood of scorn,
On this Walpurgis Night
Cloven hoofed the thirteen sing,
Unlock the gates to hell
All's inverted time stands still,
The mist of treason forms
Release the burning flames of hate,
Set free the unknown beast
Evil reigns, prepare for pain,
Demons stalk for prey
The beast of sin has been reborn,
On this Walpurgis Night

Eden Lies Obscured

Brooding winds speak of mourning shadows,
Graying skies plague the day
Dark angels haunt the passing of twilight,
Arise the legions of pain
Bound by darkness the serpent breeds evil,
Forbidden truths have been shown
Death walks side by side with the exiled,
Shamed are the parents of man
Behind the clouds of a million dark nightmares,
Resplendent beauty decays
Beyond its gates wither dreams of redemption,
And Eden lies obscured
Cursed at birth by the burden of failure,
Each generation is flawed
The myth of hope, disappears in the night winds,
And Eden is no more

Night Terror

All this darkness looks the same,
Deceiving that which dreams
Nocturnal slumber paralyzed,
Nightmares come alive
Creatures from the shaded light,
With dripping lips, desire
Terrorize each frozen breath,
With panicked, screamless eyes
The hope of morning, never comes,
A stagnant kiss, erodes
Gripped by torments shadowed gaze,
Labored breath respires

Printed in the United States
By Bookmasters

Printed in the United States
By Bookmasters